POPULAR PIANO SOLOS

Pop Hits, Broadway, Movies and More!

ISBN 978-1-4234-0906-9

Exclusively Distributed By

HAL•LEONARD®

Visit Hal Leonard Online at
www.halleonard.com

Contact Us:
Hal Leonard
7777 West Bluemound Road
Milwaukee, WI 53213
Email: info@halleonard.com

In Europe contact:
Hal Leonard Europe Limited
Distribution Centre, Newmarket Road
Bury St Edmunds, Suffolk, IP33 3YB
Email: info@halleonardeurope.com

In Australia contact:
Hal Leonard Australia Pty. Ltd.
4 Lentara Court
Cheltenham, Victoria, 3192 Australia
Email: info@halleonard.com.au

Contents

Yesterday

Use with John Thompson's Modern Course for the Piano
THIRD GRADE BOOK, after page 5.

Words and Music by John Lennon
and Paul McCartney
Arranged by Glenda Austin

Like a music box, not rushed

With light pedal

Beauty and the Beast

from Walt Disney's BEAUTY AND THE BEAST

Use after page 11.

Lyrics by Howard Ashman
Music by Alan Menken
Arranged by Glenda Austin

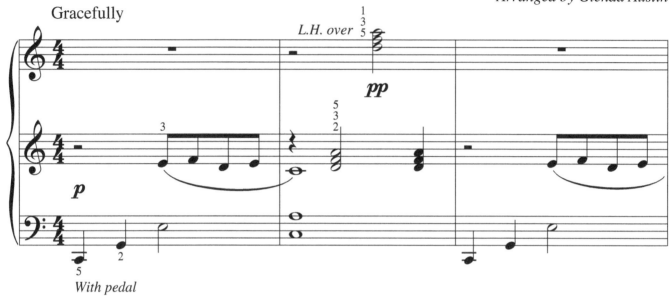

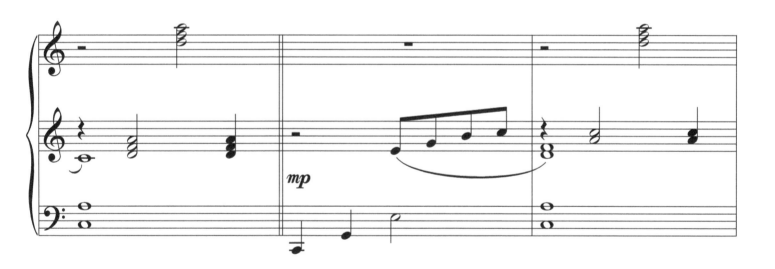

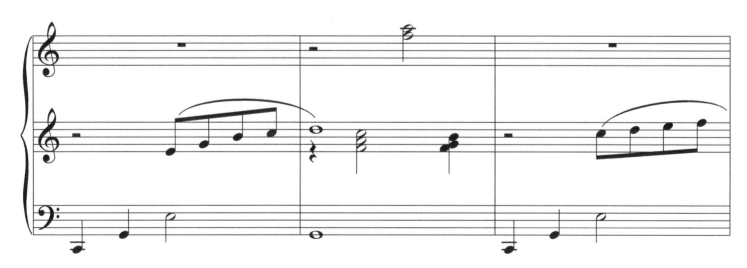

molto rit.

f a tempo

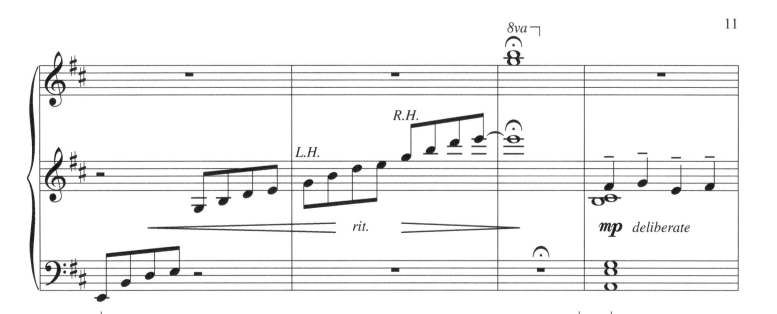

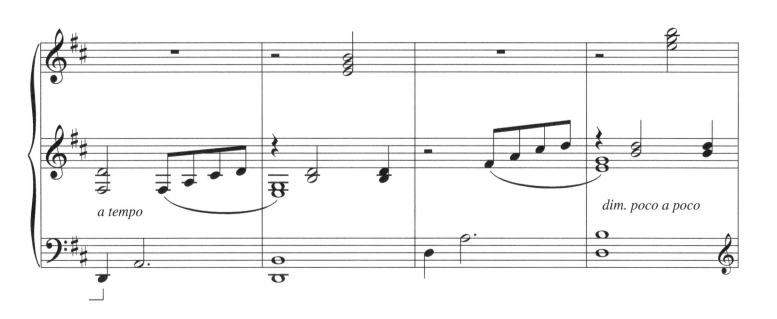

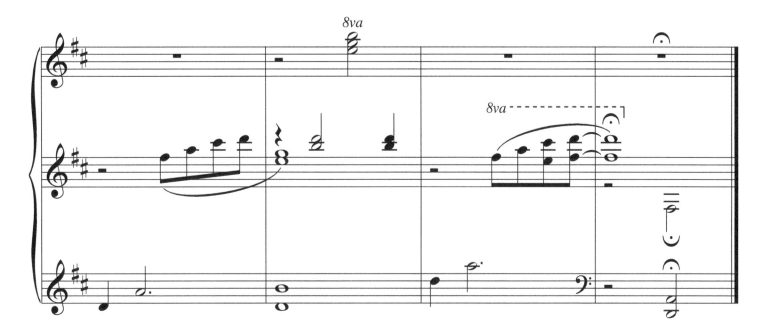

Getting to Know You

from THE KING AND I

Use after page 18.

Lyrics by Oscar Hammerstein II
Music by Richard Rodgers
Arranged by Glenda Austin

Lightly, with a lilt

Tomorrow
from the Musical Production ANNIE
Use after page 21.

Lyric by Martin Charnin
Music by Charles Strouse
Arranged by Glenda Austin

Cheerfully, with optimism!

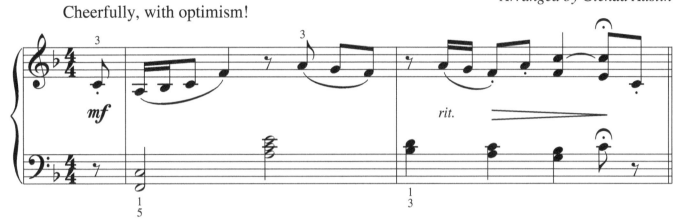

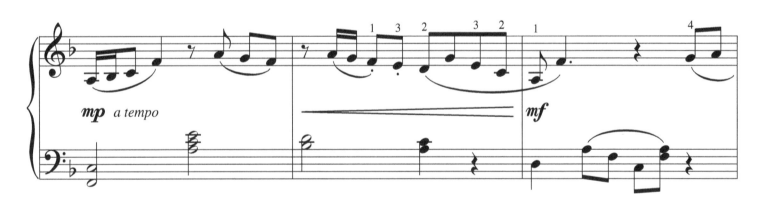

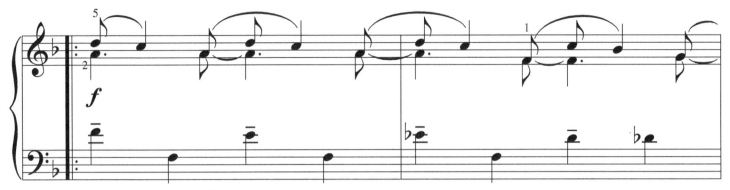

light pedal, if desired

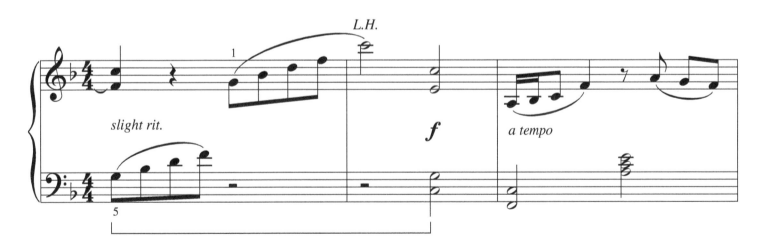

slight rit.   *L.H.*   *f*   *a tempo*

rit.

Castle on a Cloud
from LES MISÉRABLES
Use after page 24.

Music by Claude-Michel Schönberg
Lyrics by Alain Boublil, Jean-Marc Natel
and Herbert Kretzmer
Arranged by Glenda Austin

Not rushed, wistfully

Medley from
The Phantom of the Opera
Use after page 31.

Music by Andrew Lloyd Webber
Lyrics by Charles Hart
Additional Lyrics by Richard Stilgoe
Arranged by Glenda Austin

With much feeling

With pedal

THINK OF ME

THE MUSIC OF THE NIGHT

ALL I ASK OF YOU

Goodnight, My Someone

from Meredith Willson's THE MUSIC MAN

Use after page 49.

By Meredith Willson
Arranged by Glenda Austin

slight rit.

p

a tempo

Bring out L.H. melody

The Glory of Love

Use after page 61.

Words and Music by Billy Hill
Arranged by Glenda Austin

Not too fast, with a swing

Climb Ev'ry Mountain

from THE SOUND OF MUSIC

Use after page 75.

Lyrics by Oscar Hammerstein II
Music by Richard Rodgers
Arranged by Glenda Austin

Bibbidi-Bobbidi-Boo
(The Magic Song)
from Walt Disney's CINDERELLA
Use after page 80.

Words by Jerry Livingston
Music by Mack David and Al Hoffman
Arranged by Glenda Austin

Light and carefree